NOW YOU SEE

NEW CHINESE VIDEO ART FROM THE COLLECTION OF DR. MICHAEL I. JACOBS

Edited by Chrissie Iles

with contributions by Melissa Chiu and Robin Peckham

CONTENTS

FOREWORD
Tony Guerrero

Whitebox Art Center is honored to host *Now You See: Chinese Video Art from the Collection of Dr. Michael I. Jacobs*. The exhibition is a uniquely personal engagement, as it draws from Dr. Jacobs' growing collection and his experiences with young Chinese video artists in recent years. Dr. Jacobs' commitment to the medium and the artists is evidenced in his nine voyages to China, where he navigated the transformative landscape of new video art.

I am happy to celebrate this introduction to a younger generation of Chinese artists, as my own story of contemporary art begins with their predecessors. As an assistant to the estimable artist Chen Zhen more than twenty years ago, I was introduced to "les amis chinois," as Chen used to say—Cai Guo Qiang, Wenda Gu, Yan Pei Ming, Xu Bing, and Huang Yong Ping, among others. Chen's perspective, as a Chinese artist establishing himself in the Western art world, opened my eyes to the richness of art coming out of China.

Now You See invites us to open our eyes once more, reinforcing the bridges between China and the rest of the world that have been built through increased access to the Internet, the proliferation of social media, and the sharing of ideas in educational exchanges. As these connections are strengthened, the young Chinese artists in this exhibition assert themselves as an affirmation of a movement of contemporary video art that deserves our attention.

We at Whitebox Art Center are very grateful to Dr. Michael I. Jacobs and to Chrissie Iles for their enthusiasm for this project, and for the opportunity to enjoy our shared passion for Chinese video art.

ACKNOWLEDGMENTS
Michael I. Jacobs

It is my sincere hope that *Now You See: New Chinese Video Art from the Collection of Dr. Michael I. Jacobs*, through both the exhibition presented at Whitebox Art Center in New York from May 25 to June 19, 2014, and this catalogue, will raise the level of interest in these young Chinese video artists among art enthusiasts and institutions in the United States, as well as in Europe and the rest of the world. Chinese museums, both private and the government-run, are now showing contemporary Chinese video art on a regular basis, and I feel privileged to have had the opportunity to introduce these artists' work to New York. Even though they could not be present for it, the exhibition generated much excitement among the artists and has been featured on several Chinese art websites and online magazines.

First and foremost, I would like to thank all the artists who took part in this exhibition: Chen Xiaoyun, Cheng Ran, Hu Xiaoyuan, Jiang Zhi, Kan Xuan, Li Ming, Liang Yue, Liu Shiyuan, Sun Xun, and Wang Xin.

At Whitebox Art Center, New York, I am most grateful to Tony Guerrero, executive director and artistic director; Juan Puntes, founder; Igor Molochevski, manager of digital and new media technologies, and the installation team for making this important exhibition a reality. I would also like to thank Mongo Media for their technical support.

The exhibition was made possible through the generous support of Paul and Moya Coulson. Additional funding was provided by John Sichner and Robin Kellner Sichner and Anthony Orphanos.

For their insightful contributions to the catalogue, I would like to express my deepest gratitude to Dr. Melissa Chiu and Robin Peckham. Chrissie Iles was an invaluable resource and I am most grateful that she agreed to interview me for the publication. Miko McGinty designed this beautiful catalogue, assisted by Yoonjung Choi, Claire Bidwell, and Kaegan Sparks. We were fortunate to have Beth Turk assist with the editing. The entire project was managed by Tammy Leung, RN BSN. Finally, I would like to thank the following people for their help and assistance: Philip Tinari, Leo Xu, Lu Jingjing, Lorenz Hiebling, Xiyuan Zhang, and Zhang Peili in China; and in New York, Christopher Phillips and Miwako Tezuka.

INTRODUCTION
Melissa Chiu

In China, video art was always a medium used by only a few artists. In the 1990s, pioneers such as Zhang Peili, Wang GongXin, and Song Dong began to experiment with VHS videotapes. Their works were mostly documentations of performances or of their surroundings, or of dramatic events such as the destruction of the historic architecture around them in Beijing. Later that decade, a younger generation gained access to more sophisticated equipment, allowing artists such as Yang Fudong to create more cinematic productions, and Qiu Anxiong to produce stop-animation pieces set to music.

This exhibition *Now You See* represents the third generation of Chinese artists using video, incorporating all its potential for humor, social chronicle, performative gesture, and commentary. Mostly born in the 1980s and known in China as the post-1980 generation, these artists have had the benefit of a new arts education that included video. This stands in contrast to the first generation, who discovered and experimented with video privately in their studios at a time when video was not even considered an art form in China. These now senior artists have had an enormous impact on the younger generation. For example, Zhang Peili's role as a teacher at the National Art Academy in Hangzhou, where he was involved, along with Geng Jianyi, in creating a new department devoted to media arts, cannot be underestimated. This department has fostered many younger artists in their pursuit of interdisciplinary practices that include video art. One graduate of the Academy is Sun Xun, whose earliest works are included in the exhibition.

The works in the exhibition are all drawn from the collection of Dr. Michael I. Jacobs, a New York–based collector who found and acquired the work of this young generation at the beginning of their careers, before they were well known. His early recognition of the quality and importance of this new generation situates them within an international context as Dr. Jacobs' collection also includes video works by some of the most important young American and European contemporary artists working in video, including Ryan Trecartin, Nathalie Djurberg, Matt Saunders, and Korakrit Arunanondchai.

The circumstances for artists of the post-1980 generation living and working in China today could not be more different from the experiences of the two previous generations of artists. Video is now a recognized subject of study at art schools and artists today in China no longer face the same challenges, such as finding exhibition spaces to show their work, hostile government attitudes to their work sometimes resulting in censorship, access to financial support, and a market for their work. These challenges may not be completely resolved, but there are certainly more opportunities for artists today than ever before in China. Through Dr. Jacobs' prescient vision, we are able to see major examples from the current crop of artists emerging in China, at a moment when it is more and more connected to the outside world. These artists are expressing their reactions to a new set of social, environmental, personal, and cultural pressure points, each in their own way, and to great effect.

AN INTERVIEW WITH DR. MICHAEL I. JACOBS
Chrissie Iles

Chrissie Iles: Let's start at the beginning. What first drew you to China, and to Chinese art?

Dr. Michael I. Jacobs: I was invited to China by Christopher Phillips, a curator at the International Center of Photography in New York, in October 2010. I was accompanying a Board of Trustees trip, and spent a week in Beijing looking at photography, which was my main collecting focus at the time. During the trip I went exploring by myself and met young Chinese collectors as well as artists who opened their studios to me. I saw a wide range of contemporary art, including painting, sculpture, photography, and video, much of it by emerging artists.

Iles: What was it about the video work you saw during that visit that inspired you to start collecting it?

Jacobs: I was already collecting contemporary painting and sculpture, as well as video by important young American, European, and Asian artists, and I was struck by the exceptional quality of the work of young Chinese video artists. I made a second trip to China in 2010 and visited Shanghai where I saw an exhibition focused on young Chinese women artists at the Museum of Contemporary Art Shanghai. The show included three video artists who are in this exhibition: Hu Xiaoyuan, Liang Yue, and Wang Xin. I was very drawn to their vision and to their work, and tracked them down. Wang was working toward her MFA in video art at the School of the Art Institute of Chicago in the United States having graduated from the China Academy of Art in Hangzhou, where she trained under Zhang Peili, the first professor of video art in China. I contacted Wang Xin, and also went back to China to visit Zhang Peili in Hangzhou later that summer. He organized a studio visit tour for me that included young video artists as well as his former students and fellow teachers at the Academy. Each of the artists I met had a unique vision and sophisticated approach to the medium of video that equaled anything I had seen in the West. I decided to accept Whitebox Art Center's invitation to make this exhibition because I wanted to see these young Chinese video artists become more visible outside China, and especially to be seen in New York.

Iles: What is it about China and its culture that you find compelling?

Jacobs: China is at the forefront of the future. It is changing rapidly economically, socially, and culturally. New museums are opening every month, most recently the Sifang Art Museum in Nanjing and several museums in Shanghai: the two branches of the Long Museum, which together are bigger than most museums in the United States, the Power Station of Art, China's first state-run contemporary art museum, and the Yuz Museum, which opened in May 2014. All over China collectors are starting to build museums to both display their collections and show traveling exhibitions from within China and from abroad.

The Chinese audience for contemporary art is currently a small group of dedicated individuals. Over time, the number of collectors, art enthusiasts, and young people discovering art for the first time will further expand the audience. As society opens up and the middle class grows in both size and wealth, more Chinese people are beginning to travel for the first time and are discovering what is happening in the rest of the world culturally at the same moment that China is developing its own contemporary culture and an independent art world. One of the striking things about China is the way in which it constantly renews itself. It has managed to move through an ideological revolution and begin the transformation that it must now make in order to move away from its past and into the current millennium, producing strong contemporary art and culture with a level of sophistication and openness that is exemplified by all the video works in this exhibition. Each video expresses a clear, independent voice that engages with the history of China, current issues, and personal artistic concerns in a way that does not rely on a Western vocabulary of art, yet resonates strongly with it. The existence of such a strong contemporary art scene in China, despite its small audience, says something very important about China itself. It has not flourished simply because of the possibilities it generates for the art market.

Iles: You witnessed that sea change as it was happening, arriving in China at a moment when these new ideas were being expressed for the first time by this third generation of Chinese video artists. Maybe the reason that video is so powerful in their hands is that it is such a contemporary medium. It also allows ideas to be expressed in a performative way, connecting us to the body at a moment when perceptions of the body in the West are becoming increasingly dematerialized through the Internet. In the animation films in your collection we can also see how traditional mediums in Chinese art, such as calligraphy, woodblock printing, and scroll painting, have been used to great effect in a contemporary way, transforming the language of traditional Chinese political propaganda to ask serious questions about what's going on in contemporary China.

In this globalized, somewhat homogenized world of images, you arrived in China and understood the power of this current cultural moment there, suspended somewhere between the old regime, in which things were highly restricted, and what the current technological and social transformation is leading toward. Chinese art is becoming increasingly connected to the rest of the world, and that will inevitably change the way in which Chinese artists make their work. The videos in your collection all articulate a moment somewhere between the past and the future—a very creative moment,

not yet overexposed to the Internet and the global commercialized visual culture that saturates the West.

This hybrid of the old communist system and high capitalism has produced a generation of artists that you found just as they were emerging, and you acted very precisely in that moment. You didn't wait for their work to be endorsed by museums, critics, other collectors, or the market; you acted as all great collectors act, using your instinct and your eye. This bold and decisive approach is what distinguishes the shape of your collection in general, and this part of your collection in particular. One of the striking things about the group of works that you have brought together is how different they are, yet how strongly they resonate with each other.

Jacobs: I agree. What unites them, for me, is the extraordinary visual imagination of the artists. Wang Xin's video *Diffraction* (2010), a slow, almost forensic study of found objects, is very sculptural, and draws our attention to the process of looking. Kan Xuan's *Jumping Taste* (2011) animates a photograph of the head of a Chinese woman in traditional costume inside a grid of circles; by referencing graphic design from traditional political Chinese propaganda and overlaying it with the grammar of commercial advertising, Kan Xuan subverts the conventions of both and creates a third space that implies the possibility for the existence of an independent artistic voice. There are four animation films by Sun Xun in the exhibition, all socially and politically engaged moral tales that critique Chinese politics and the system using a dark, psychological narrative structure. I was impressed by Sun Xun's poetic approach to his rigorous subject matter. *Beyond-ism* (2010), for example, centers on "Snow," a poem written in 1936 by Mao Zedong that makes evident the political ambitions of the man who would go on to found the People's Republic of China. After praising the beauty of the northern Chinese landscape in winter, Mao dismisses the great emperors of the past, proclaiming that the true hero (himself) is only just about to appear. In Sun Xun's film Mao's poem appears as a written text that fills the screen, over which insects crawl. A dragon, traditionally a symbol of power and good luck and, more specifically, of the Emperor of China, appears wafting through a watery background as bats circle an abandoned colonial building. Ravens gather; emperors float in the night sky, blown by the wind. All these ghostly images evoke the memory of faded power. At the end of the film, insects cover the screen until the light becomes obliterated. Each of Sun Xun's films takes a different graphic approach, combining techniques of traditional Chinese scroll painting and graphic art with Western animation and comic-book styles. It was clear to me from the beginning that he is a major talent in Chinese art, and his work is now becoming recognized internationally, by both museums and film festivals.

I am also struck by the way in which this bold, poetic approach is also expressed through performance in a number of the video works in the collection. As we know, performance is very popular in the West at the moment, and I think that is partly because, in a world dominated by the Internet, people have a strong desire to be together and experience something in real time and space. In China the Internet is not as dominant, yet artists there are equally drawn to performance. I am drawn to their fresh approach and expression of it through the medium of video. I think Chinese video artists sense that their experience of time, and of physical space, is being altered by the myriad of changes that are occurring around them. In *Comb* (2008), for example, Li Ming is expressing his reaction to the rapid destruction of historic Chinese architecture and the communities that it housed, which has occurred in recent years in China as new cities have been built. In the video, a mechanical digger can be seen smashing a hole in an old building and slowly advancing into a room in which a young Chinese woman sits motionless, with her back to the camera. The mechanical digger gently reaches its long arm towards the back of her head in an almost human gesture, as though trying to connect with the person whose historic environment it is destroying.

Jiang Zhi, one of the two older artists in the exhibition, along with Chen Xiaoyuan, who has been underrepresented in the Chinese video art world, made *Fly, Fly* (1997) addressing a similar issue almost ten years earlier during a period of major political and cultural change in China. Jiang Zhi belongs to China's second generation of video artists who emerged during this period, and his work articulates the turbulent changes in Chinese society that occurred then, and the feelings of alienation that these changes produced. In *Fly, Fly*, Jiang Zhi holds a video camera in his right hand and films his left hand flapping like the wings of a bird as he moves around his cramped apartment in Beijing. A soundtrack of classical music from Massenet's opera *Thaïs* evokes a fantasy of experiencing another, Western world, the impossibility of which Jiang Zhi's futile gesture of flying makes evident.

I find it interesting to see how this approach has developed in Jiang Zhi's more recent work. Another of his videos in the exhibition, *0.7% Salt* (2009), addresses the politics of watching in the current media environment, in which popular culture is exerting an increasing power. A famous young Chinese actress performs for Jiang Zhi, sitting motionless in front of the camera, gradually breaking out of her public persona and dissolving into tears. Jiang Zhi's instructions to the actress shift her engagement with the camera from her familiar professional acting experience to a performative action that triggered the memory of a major trauma in her personal life, when her ex-boyfriend posted explicit pictures of her on the Internet, derailing her career. Jiang Zhi's video is a moving study of the destructive potential of the Internet, and the ethical issues raised by its erosion of the boundary between public and private life. It is striking to see how both his early and more recent work articulate a sense of emotional frustration through a simple yet moving performative action.

Liu Shiyuan's *Evidence* (2009) is perhaps the closest in style to Western performative video; yet it retains a uniquely Chinese sensibility. The artist invited a group of friends to a party in her studio and asked them to bring items of clothing that symbolized their personal identities. She attached a number to each item of clothing and asked each person to randomly pick a number and try on the clothing corresponding to that number. Each person then chose a number to which the artist had assigned an action she associated with the identity of each person feeling jealous, fighting, kissing, dancing and acted out that action, creating a multiple exchange of roles. The walls of the studio, painted in different colors, framed the actions within a painterly tableau, as the highly emotive actions performed by each person presented an exploratory freedom of identity unthinkable in the restrictive ideological and social norms of Chinese society. Unlike some Western contemporary video, which appropriates only the style of 1970s performance, Liu Shiyuan's response to social constriction is actually parallel to that expressed by 1970s Western artists using video during that period, but using the language of contemporary art.

In *Drag* (2006), Chen Xiaoyun, who, like Jiang Zhi is in his early forties, uses the performative body in a very different way, evoking both Western 1970s body art and Chinese martial arts, with a dramatic use of cinematic light and shadow. Chen Xiaoyun's videos are raw and direct, using the camera to create sharply edited gestural works. In *Drag*, a shirtless man appears pulling a rope, struggling against an opponent hidden from view in a darkened room. The camera pans out to reveal his shadow looming against the wall, wearing a pointed hat and alternately pulling the rope and allowing it to become slack. The second half of the video is composed of rapidly edited movements of the magician-like figure, in a semi-abstract composition of shadowy gestures whose expressionistic form suggests a struggle with an internal, or maybe external, invisible force.

Again and again, I have been struck by the boldness of these young artists, and the clarity of their creative response to their environment. Cheng Ran, who was born in Inner Mongolia, made a video titled *Rock Dove* (2009), in which homing pigeons can be seen roosting in the roof of an old factory building crisscrossed with water pipes, which for Cheng Ran represent the circulatory system of the social body. Suddenly the neon lights hanging from the ceiling are switched on and off repeatedly, disturbing the equilibrium of the space and sending the pigeons into a panicked flight around the room, illuminated by the dramatic flashing between light and dark. Like so many of the video artists in the collection, Cheng Ran uses the camera to create a haunting visual narrative that addresses the disruption of a community by an unseen technological presence.

Cheng Ran's new video *Simply Wild* (2014), receiving its world premiere in this exhibition, deals with another aspect of technology's influence: the impact of the Internet on how lovers communicate. As a beautiful woman appears moving through a city, her ex-lover tries to reconnect with her in a series of texts that appear scrolling down the left-hand side of the screen. Cheng Ran worked for the artist Yang Fudong, helping to film his early works and also appearing as an actor in some of his movies. The cinematographic, grainy quality of the video, which was shot on Super-8 film, sets up a romantic mood, which is heightened by the longing expressed by the ex-lover, whose emotional messages appear almost like subtitles in a 1970s French New Wave movie, yet are clumsy and inept in their attempts to win her over.

I perceived a similar sensibility in Liang Yue's *Stop Dazing* (2004), a poetic narrative that unfolds like a dream. We see streets at night; rain on the windshield of a car; tiny, colored fairy lights blurred and magnified. A spoken narrative appears in subtitled translation, leading us through a series of memories, images, and moments that seem removed from the present, yet not located in any specific moment. Liang Yue narrates her journey through the Chinese metropolis where she lives, interspersing her footage with children's drawings, text, and photographs to create an intimate portrait of an inner world.

The visual and creative power of all these works spoke to me very directly. Many of the videos were made when the artists were in their twenties, at the beginning of their careers, and as part of practices that also included other media, including sculpture, painting, drawing, and photography. This is clearly reflected in the different ways in which they use the medium of video; their images are painterly, graphic, sculptural, photographic, performative, and cinematic. This is why I would like to see this generation of Chinese artists on the world stage alongside the other important young video artists emerging in the West, the Middle East, and in Asia.

Iles: I agree. This exhibition makes very clear how vital it is to see this work in a wider context, because it is an important part of the global dialogue. Even though the Internet remains restricted to the artists on certain levels, they are engaging with it in a very intelligent way. They are also engaging with cinema, which has been a significant cultural influence in China, particularly since the end of the Cultural Revolution in the late 1970s. Some of this work is arguably creating a new kind of hybrid cinematic language that incorporates Chinese poetry and literature as well as narrative cinema within the framework of video art.

Jacobs: It is interesting to see how this engage-ment has developed as the access to Western movies and to international contemporary art has slowly increased, and artists have been able to travel outside China and take part in residency programs and international exhibitions.

Iles: Exhibitions are one of the key ways in which art becomes visible. How do you see this exhibition in relation to other exhibitions of Chinese video art that have taken place?

Jacobs: There have been two important exhibitions that have made contemporary Chinese video art more visible in the United States: *Between Past and Future: New Photography and Video from China* (2004), curated by Wu Hung and Christopher Phillips and co-organized by the International Center of Photography, New York, and the David and Alfred Smart Museum of Art, University of Chicago, in collaboration with the Asia Society, New York, which included one artist in this exhibition, Jiang Zhi; and the first exhibition devoted to Chinese video art in the United States, *Perspectives 180 - Unfinished Country: New Video Art from China* (2012), which was presented at the Contemporary Art Museum in Houston and Asia Society Texas Center and was curated by James Elaine, a former curator at the Hammer Museum in Los Angeles.

In China, the Minsheng Art Museum in Shanghai presented *Moving Image in China 1988–2011* in the fall of 2011, a very important show that included seventy video works by sixty-one artists. The exhibition was a compendium of Chinese video art, from the earliest works made by the first video art professors in China to recent work by several young artists. This exhibition was followed in January 2013 by a show of commissioned works by fifty young Chinese artists and artist groups at the Ullens Center for Contemporary Art in Beijing, *ON | OFF: China's Young Artists in Concept and Practice*, curated by Bao Dong and Sun Dongdong, and supervised by Philip Tinari, the director of the center. Some of the artists in both of these presen-tations are represented in my collection and are part of this exhibition.

And in Europe, an exhibition of recent Chinese video art, titled *PANDAMONIUM: Media Art from Shanghai*, curated by David Elliott and Li Zhenhua, took place in early 2014 at Momentum Berlin, which co-organized the show with the Chronus Art Center Shanghai. Elliott also curated one of the first exhibitions of contemporary Chinese art in the West, *Silent Energy*, at the Museum of Modern Art, in Oxford, England, in 1990.

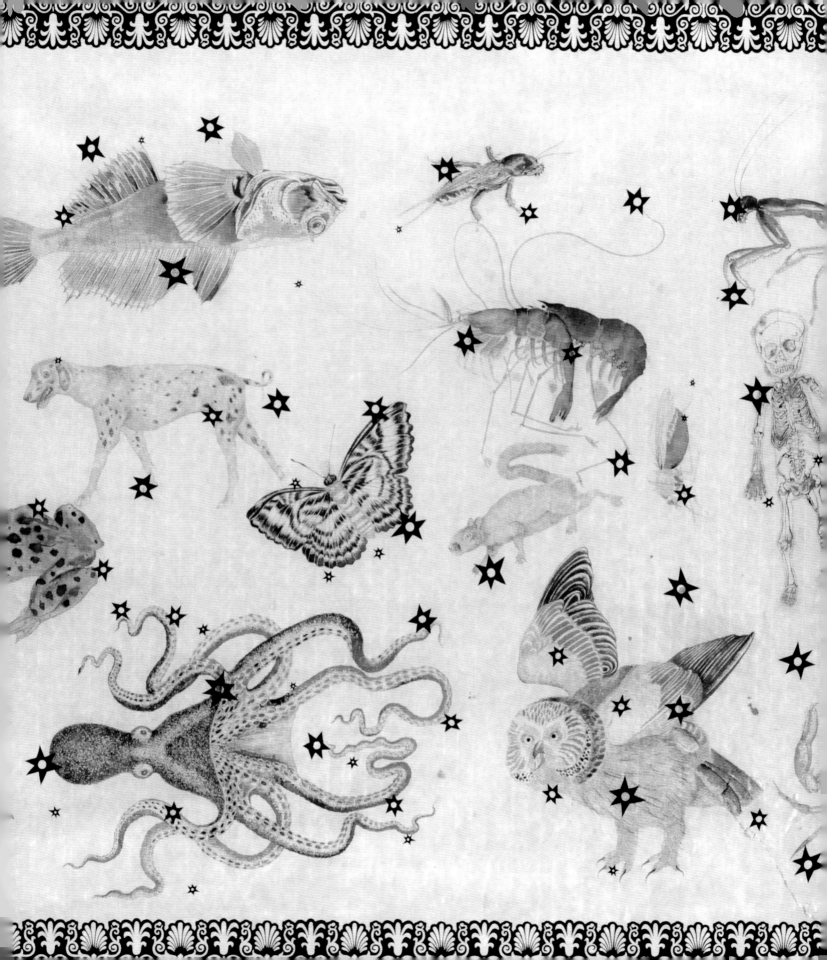

NOW YOU SEE
Robin Peckham

Video art first appeared in China in such a direct and confrontational way that its earliest practitioners were able to set the rules of their medium almost immediately. When Zhang Peili premiered *30 x 30* at a conference of artists in 1988, showing a recording of himself breaking and repairing a small square mirror over the complete course of a videotape, he ensured that the discussion about this new medium would be about performance, boredom, minimalism, violence. This is the conceptual core around which practices in video and electronic art would orbit over the decade to come—and yet, in so many ways, it offers only one specific example of how video has been integrated into the contemporary art world and the lives of young people in China. In parallel, the collection of Dr. Michael I. Jacobs focuses on another narrative of Chinese video, one that could be positioned in a generational light (while Zhang Peili was born in 1957, lived through the Cultural Revolution, and led the '85 New Wave movement, the oldest artists here, Jiang Zhi and Chen Xiaoyun, were born in 1971, and came of age in a consumer society). Rather than working in such broad historical strokes, however, it pays to think less about identity and more about the pleasures of exploration, and why younger artists might feel the need to work through the imagery of their present in a visually and intellectually distinct way.

Jiang Zhi belongs to the first wave of artists to use video in a way that was fundamentally different from the premises set out by Zhang Peili's generation, and this is no accident. Jiang first emerged as a journalist and designer working for Jiedao, a Shenzhen-based magazine of urbanism and street culture that helped reinvent the way artists in the Pearl River Delta, the massive agglomeration of cities spanning Guangzhou and its neighbors used as a testing ground for new economic policies in the 1990s, thought about youth culture and the everyday. By 1996 he had moved to Beijing and had acquired some rudimentary video equipment at a flea market under the influence of his former classmates Yang Fudong, who had already begun making art films, and the slightly older Qiu Zhijie, whose recorded experiments with his body largely bridged the gap between these two generations. What Jiang Zhi did with his camera, however, was somehow more casual, more youthful, and more hopeful: in 1997 he recorded *Fly, Fly*, holding the camera in his right hand while filming his left as it flapped like the wings of a bird around his apartment. It is a simple gesture, but one that lets into the frame everything that artists like Zhang Peili or even Qiu Zhijie insisted on excluding from their early video works: the mess of the studio (or, in this case, apartment), the emotions of the artist, and the imperfections of the medium. This was video art for artists who had been working in amateur photography, people for whom television was something more (if just barely) than a form of institutional propaganda.

There is something very real and raw in Jiang Zhi's early work (and other videos of the same era, like Yan Lei's *1500cm* [1995] or Qiu Zhijie's *Bathroom* [1997]), and it is this intensity that he and his peers learned to capture through sharply edited, short, gestural works in the ensuing decade. Chen Xiaoyun, an early accomplice of Jiang Zhi, captures this feeling in *Drag* (2006), which depicts a shirtless man pulling vigorously against a rope, the other end of which is held by a figure in a magician's (or dunce's) cap who is viewed only in shadow. As Chen Xiaoyun becomes further seduced by narrative—and its disruption—he also turns towards complicated systems of symbols: in *Why Life* (2010), short texts and video vignettes flash across three screens, searching for poignant images but ending up with so many of them that the project becomes a terrifying procession of encounters.

This turn towards high style and complex narratives is most fully realized in the work of younger artists like Cheng Ran and Huang Ran, who shoot works in video that are often read as cinema, competing occasionally with the slick production values of senior artists like Yang Fudong (who was indeed a mentor to Cheng). Unlike in the West, in China video was not immediately understood as an alternative value system to television or as an affordable substitute for film; instead, it was immediately implicated in both systems of circulation, as some of Zhang Peili's most central works of the early- and mid-1990s both hired TV news anchors as actors (*Water*, 1992) and remixed classic propaganda films (*Last Words*, 2003). As a conceptual possibility, this might be traced to the relative immaturity of local cinematic and televisual cultures. Indeed, it falls to artists like Cheng Ran to produce what could otherwise appear as art film. In many of his films, it is not the narrative but rather the editing and directorial technique that plays with this effect—and a massive lust for the theatrical. In *Rock Dove* (2009), cameras cut and pan across pigeons in trees, right up until huge banks of fluorescent lights illuminate the scene, which is revealed to take place on a soundstage. Here, artifice and its revelation are brought together in a span of moments whereas in longer productions like the four-channel *Sorrows of Young Werther* (2008), they are bound up in the experience of viewing a film that seems to be fully self-aware that it is, in fact, an installation.

Of course, stylistic mannerism and outlandish narrative are not the sole province of artists with an abiding interest in the traditions of the European art house or Chinese propaganda in the form of the moving image. Both Sun Xun and Ye Linghan have developed incredibly intricate systems in animation, with the former in particular drawing on ink painting as a cultural resource that, combined with the historical analyses of ideological movements and top-down politics that have become the province of both, proffers a devastating critique of contemporary amnesia in society at large and in contemporary art itself. Sun Xun's *Some Actions which Haven't Been Defined Yet in the Revolution* (2011), for instance, gestures back to the politicized

woodblock iconography of the Republican era, building a new mythology for the basis of what art has become today.

If considered composition and narrative plotting represent one of the directions that has grown out of the gestural 1990s video of figures like Jiang Zhi, Qiu Zhijie, and Yan Lei, another more significant branch would be the methodology (or at least aesthetic) of the experiment. While these would appear to be opposing strategies, they often boil down to a much simpler question: whether the conceptual framework of video as practice should be revealed within or left outside of the completed work. One of the most interesting voices in this category is Liu Shiyuan. The video *Evidence* (2009) is a surprising twist for the artist, who generally works on more formal questions of photography and the globalization of representation; this work finds her organizing a party at which her friends swap clothes and enact identities fabricated based on their new outfits. The result contains shades of Cao Fei and Ryan Trecartin alike, but ultimately remains rooted in an everyday sensibility within the confines of an experimental form of play. Here the complexity of her resulting story, extemporaneous as it is, comes full circle and rejoins the careful narrative of an artist like Cheng Ran. Wang Xin, who works most explicitly in the new media paradigm espoused by her former mentor Zhang Peili, often works on the edges of video and has been known to set up socially engineered situations not unlike this one; see, for instance, Wang's brilliant *Asterism* (2014). Trained and practicing abroad, like Liu Shiyuan, Wang Xin also has an appreciation for the subtlety of the gesture. *Diffraction: Objects* (2010) begins with a physical meditation over a series of objects brought into relationship with one another: glass beads in the angles of a pinecone, a magnifying glass over an old photograph.

Pushing these contrived, experimental situations to their limits, some of the most exciting artists today work in a voice that is almost immediately identifiable with the raw gestures of Yan Lei and Jiang Zhi, albeit in a way that is significantly more humorous in its approach, more sarcastic in its tone, more knowing in its approach to global art history, and more carefree in relation to its own position in the Chinese art world. Li Ran, Chen Zhou, and Hu Xiangqian are strong examples here with their language play, dry humor, and brutally affected naivete, but it is Li Ming who has most precisely perfected the strategy. In *Comb* (2008), the arm of a backhoe reaches through a demolished brick wall and tenderly attempts to stroke the long, disheveled hair of a figure facing away from the camera; in *XX* (2009), two men attempt to exchange a shirt while maintaining constant skin-on-skin contact; in *Songs of the Artist* (2011), two geese are tied together at the neck and forced to learn to get along together (the reader will not be surprised to learn that Li Ming and his galleries have received even more animal cruelty complaints than Lu Yang and hers, but he appears less amenable to surrender). Li Ming and his peers have recaptured a sheer energy that has been missing from Chinese video since its initial explorations in performance were co-opted by the self-serious endurance efforts of body art in the 1990s.

Also notable in this respect is Hu Xiaoyuan, one of the few artists included here not working primarily let alone exclusively in video and other lens-based media. Known for her delicate efforts in painting and sculpture, often combining silk and wood grain, Hu Xiaoyuan has surprised at many of her recent exhibition appearances with crushingly funny and materially alluring video works, including *No Reason Why* (2010): what looks to be a silkworm cocoon slowly wriggles around the frame for twenty-odd minutes, occasionally seeming to breathe or pulsate in places. All about the body and yet remaining cunningly ungendered (and even inhuman), the work suggests a touch of the emotional or even sentimental. Kan Xuan, on the other hand, keeps the body gestured but unsexualized, as with *A Happy Girl* (2002), in which a naked body suddenly appears on a pedestal in a backyard, or *Looking for looking for* (2001), in which a tightly framed spider roams the contours of naked bodies.

By contrast to the common misunderstanding that young Chinese art is focused on the personal and the everyday, a brief survey of video in the 2000s handily demonstrates that political critique, theatrical scriptwriting, rigorous experimentation, and biting humor are all alive and well. In many ways this represents an extremely diverse cross-section of individual practices that spans a broad spectrum of strategies and approaches: high production values vie with low, popular culture is set against independent film, and performative gestures sit alongside complex cinematic narratives. As rich as this scene is, it is tempting to conclude that many of these positions actually constitute responses to, radicalizations of, and reactions against the style of video first defined by Zhang Peili in the closing years of the 1980s. If this is the case, however, and Zhang Peili's school of thinking remains the invisible nucleus around which all of this revolves, then it has been modulated by a polyphony of other voices from within China and beyond. What remains striking is that, as much as Chinese video now interacts with a variety of global discourses in art, cinema, and performance, it also functions as a relatively isolated and self-contained conversation, drawing in ideas from elsewhere but stubbornly—and productively—refusing to simply become a strain of what video now means in the contemporary art world at large. In this way young Chinese video art today remains true to its roots in Hangzhou of the 1980s, and yet has become something so much more: a hand flying around a cramped room, but also an airplane.

Chen Xiaoyun

Drag, 2006. Single-channel color video, silent. 4:11 min.

Cheng Ran
Rock Dove, 2009. Single-channel color video, sound. 5 min.

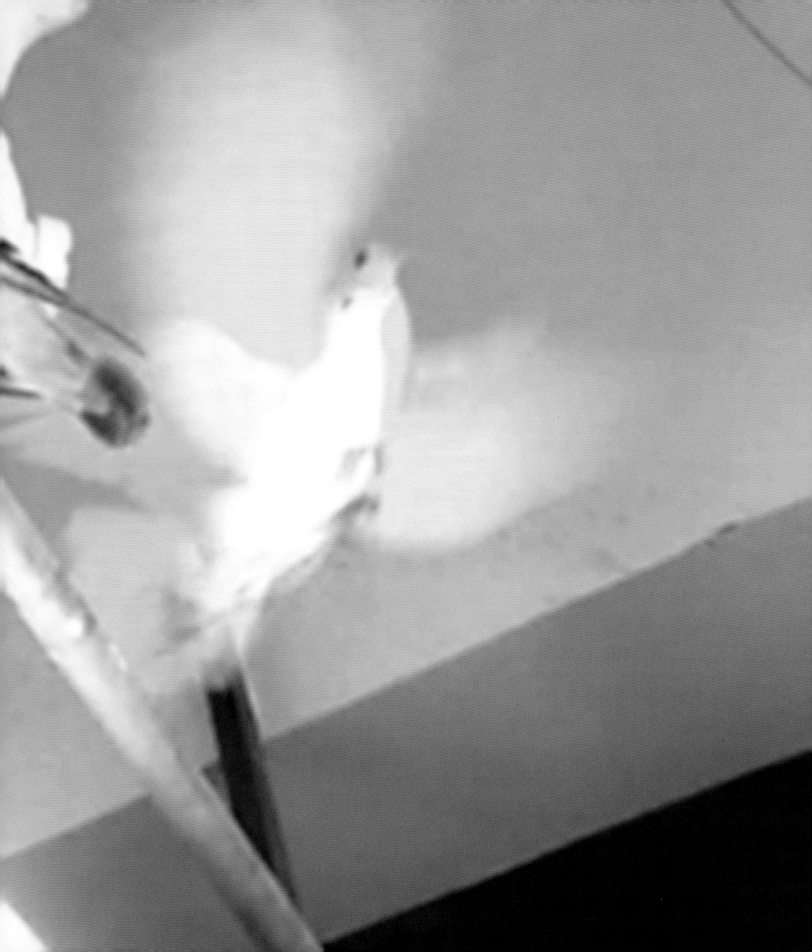

Cheng Ran

The Sorrows of Young Werther, 2009. 4-channel color video, sound. 10:12 min.

Cheng Ran
Anonymity, or Imitation and Imagining of Man Ray's Tears (1930–1932), 2010. Single-channel color video, sound. 15 min.

I remember

when we chatted
u told me
u thought i was cute
and
u
wanted to chill...

In case
u dont know
who this is its ME ..

Cheng Ran
Simply Wild, 2014. Single-channel color video, sound. 5 min.

i

understand

but

its

really

the only palce

to find

Hu Xiaoyuan
No Reason Why, 2010. Single-channel color video, sound. 22 min.

Jiang Zhi
0.7% Salt, 2009. Single-channel color video, silent. 8:35 min.

Jiang Zhi

Fly, Fly, 1997. Single-channel black-and-white video, sound. 5:15 min.

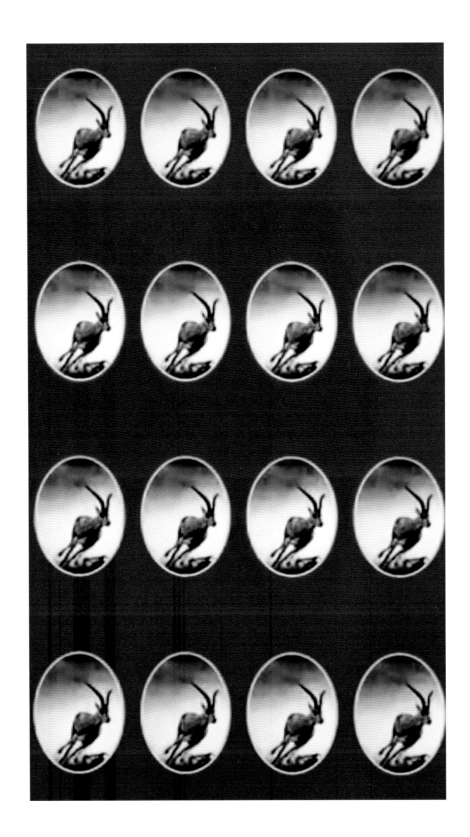

Kan Xuan
Jumping Taste, 2011. Single-channel color video, sound. 2:14 min.

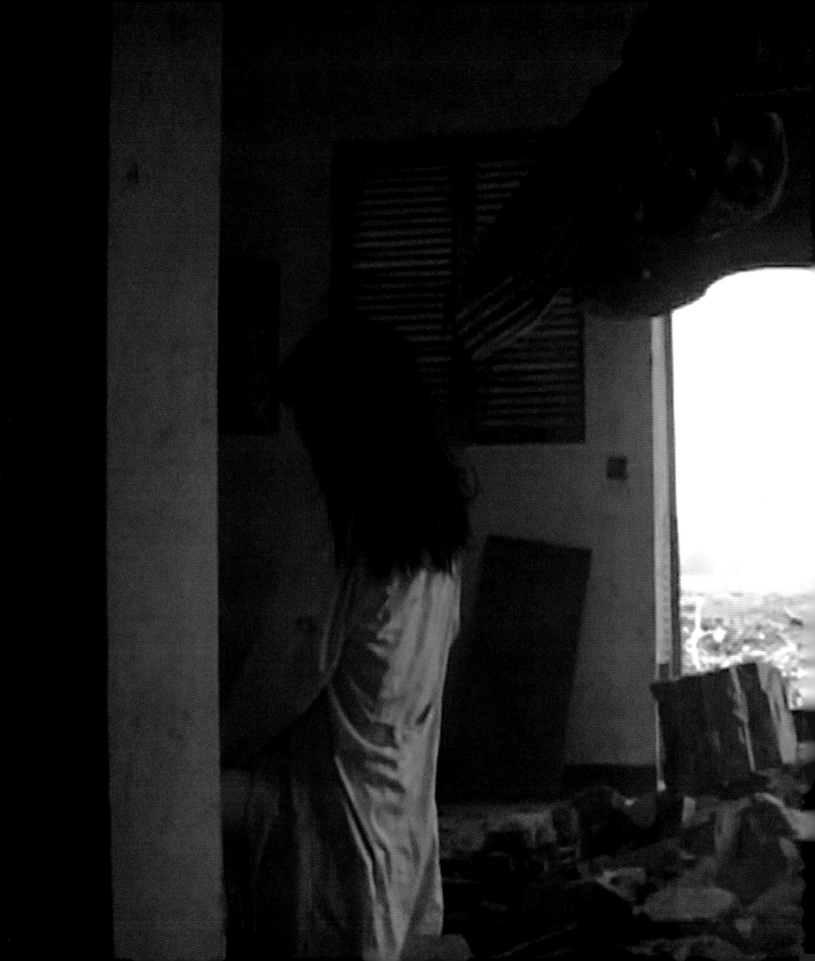

Li Ming
Comb, 2008. Single-channel color video, sound. 7:15 min.

Li Ming
Swordsman-HA HA HA HA HA, 2011. Single-channel color video, sound. 3:27 min.

Liang Yue
Stop Dazing, 2004. Single-channel color video, sound. 35:35 min.

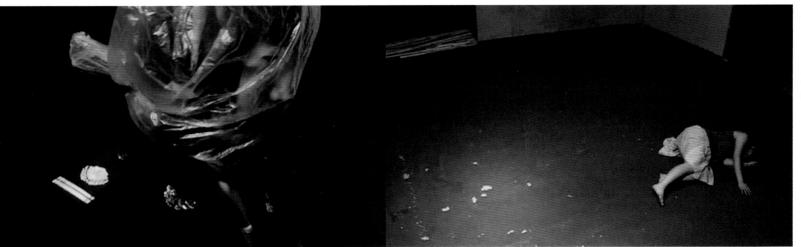

Liu Shiyuan
Evidence, 2009. Single-channel color video, sound. 11:39 min.

Sun Xun

People's Republic of Zoo, 2009. Single-channel color video, sound. 7:30 min.

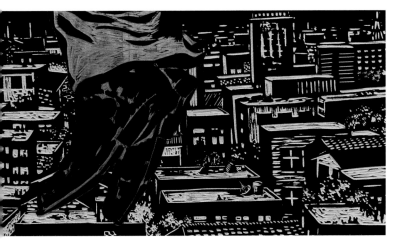 

Sun Xun
Some Actions which Haven't Been Defined Yet in the Revolution, 2010. Single-channel color video, sound. 12:22 min.

Sun Xun
Heroes No Longer, 2010. Single-channel color video, sound. 9:04 min.

英雄不再

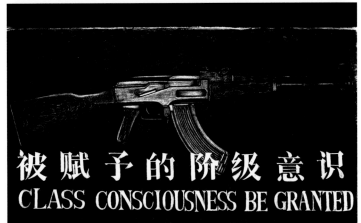

被赋予的阶级意识
CLASS CONSCIOUSNESS BE GRANTED

Sun Xun
Beyond-ism, 2010. Single-channel color video, sound. 8:08 min.

Wang Xin

Diffraction: Objects, 2010. Single-channel color video, silent. 23:19 min.

ARTISTS' BIOGRAPHIES

Chen Xiaoyun
1971 Born in Hubei Province, China
Lives and works in Beijing, China

Selected Exhibitions
2014 *Landscape: the Virtual, the Actual, the Possible?*, GuangDong Times Museum, Guangzhou, China
2011 *Moving Image in China: 1988–2011*, Minsheng Art Museum, Shanghai, China
2011 *Move on Asia: The End of Video Art (2001–2010)*, Casa Asia, Barcelona, Spain
2008 *Revolutions – Forms That Turn*, 16th Biennale of Sydney, Australia
2006 *Busan Biennale 2006*, Korea
2006 4th Seoul International Media Art Biennale (MediaCity Seoul), Seoul Museum of Art, Korea
2005 *The Second Guangzhou Triennial |BEYOND: an Extraordinary Space of Experimentation for Modernization*, Guangdong Museum of Art, Guangzhou, China
2005 *Yokohama International Triennial of Contemporary Art 2005 – Art Circus: Jumping from the Ordinary*, Yokohama, Japan

Cheng Ran
1981 Born in Inner Mongolia, China
2004 Graduated from China Academy of Art, Hangzhou, China
Lives and works in Hangzhou, China, and Amsterdam, Netherlands

Residencies
2013 Rijksakademie van Beeldende Kunsten, Amsterdam, Netherlands

Selected Exhibitions
2014 *Déjà Vu: Chinese Artists in Moving Images*, Digital Collection, Art Basel Hong Kong
2014 *Decorum*, Power Station of Art, Shanghai, China
2013 *Rewriting the Landscape: India and China*, National Museum of Modern and Contemporary Art, Gwacheon, Korea
2013 *Degeneration*, OCT Contemporary Art Terminal, Shanghai, China
2013 *West Bund 2013: A Biennial of Architecture and Contemporary Art*, Shanghai, China
2013 *ON | OFF: China's Young Artists in Concept and Practice*, Ullens Center for Contemporary Art, Beijing, China
2012 *Vídeo Guerrilha*, São Paulo, Brazil

2012 *CAFAM • Future Exhibition–Sub-Phenomena: Report on the State of Chinese Young Art*, Central Academy of Fine Arts Museum, Beijing, China
2011 *Video Art in China – MADATAC*, Museo Nacional Centro de Arte Reina Sofía, Madrid, Spain
2011 *Video Art Terminal _ Un Viatico per i Viaggiatori*, Venezia Terminal Passeggeri, Venice, Italy
2011 *Moving Image in China: 1988–2011*, Minsheng Art Museum, Shanghai, China
2009 *Cheng Ran & Jiang Pengyi: Immersion and Distance*, Ullens Center for Contemporary Art, Beijing, China
2008 *Farewell to Post-colonialism*, 3rd Guangzhou Triennial, Guangdong Museum of Art, Guangzhou, China
2008 *There Is No I in Team*, ISIS Arts and /sLab, Newcastle upon Tyne, United Kingdom
2008 *Infantization*, Taipei Museum of Contemporary Art, Taiwan

Selected Festivals and Screenings
2014 *The Exchange Program*, AVIFF–Art Film Festival, Cannes, France
2014 *Relating to*, Art Basel, Switzerland
2013 Kino Der Kunst, Munich, Germany
2013 26th European Media Art Festival, Osnabrück, Germany
2013 *An Elegy for Voice and Silence*, Art Basel Miami Beach, Florida, United States
2009 CREAM – International Festival for Arts and Media, Yokohama, Japan
2006 *Elektrische Schatten – Dokumentar- und Kurzfilme aus der VR China*, organized by Studio West, Museum der Moderne Salzburg, Austria

Hu Xiaoyuan
1977 Born in Harbin, China
2002 Graduated from the Department of Design, Central Academy of Fine Arts, Beijing, China
Lives and works in Beijing, China

Selected Exhibitions
2014 *Inside China*, Palais de Tokyo, Paris, France
2014 *Taipei Biennial 2014*, Taipei Fine Arts Museum, Taiwan
2013 *A Potent Force: Duan Jianyu and Hu Xiaoyuan*, Rockbund Art Museum, Shanghai, China
2013 *ON | OFF: China's Young Artists in Concept and Practice*, Ullens Center for Contemporary Art, Beijing, China
2012 *The Ungovernables*, 2012 New Museum Triennial, New York, United States
2012 *The 1st China–Xinjiang Contemporary Art Biennale*, Xinjiang Art Center, China
2011 *Moving Image in China 1988–2011*, Minsheng Art Museum, Shanghai, China
2010 *Beyond the Body – Contemporary Image Art Exhibition*, Museum of Contemporary Art, Shanghai, China
2010 *City States*, Liverpool Biennial 2010, Contemporary Urban Centre, United Kingdom; traveled to: Korean Cultural Centre UK, London, United Kingdom, as *Media Landscape, Zone East*
2007 *documenta 12*, Kassel, Germany

Jiang Zhi

1971 Born in Yuanjiang, China
1995 China Academy of Art, Hangzhou, China
Lives and works in Beijing and Shenzhen, China

Selected Exhibitions

2012 *Jiang Zhi: If This is a Man*, Guangdong Times Museum, Guangzhou, China
2012 *Reactivation*, 9th Shanghai Biennale, Museum of Contemporary Art, Shanghai, China
2012 *The Unseen*, 4th Guangzhou Triennial, Guangdong Museum of Art, Guangzhou, China
2011 *The 1st CAFAM Biennale: Super-Organism/Research and Experiment from a Specific View*, Central Academy of Fine Arts Museum, Beijing, China
2011 *Moving Image in China: 1988–2011*, Minsheng Art Museum, Shanghai, China
2004 *Between Past and Future: New Photography and Video from China*, International Center of Photography and Asia Society and Museum, New York, United States
2004 *Techniques of the Visible*, 2004 Shanghai Biennale, Shanghai Art Museum, China
2002 *P_A_U_S_E*, 4th Gwangju Biennale, Korea

Kan Xuan

1972 Born in Xuancheng, China
1997 BFA, China Academy of Art, Hangzhou, China
Lives and works in Amsterdam, Netherlands, and Beijing, China

Residencies

2002–3 Rijksakademie van Beeldende Kunsten, Amsterdam, Netherlands

Selected Exhibitions

2012 *Kan Xuan: Millet Mounds*, Ullens Center for Contemporary Art, Beijing, China
2008 *Insomnia*, BizArt, Shanghai, China
2008 *Our Future: The Guy and Myriam Ullens Foundation Collection*, Ullens Center for Contemporary Art, Beijing, China
2007 *Not Only Possible, But Also Necessary: Optimism in the Age of Global War*, 10th International Istanbul Biennial, Turkey
2007 *China Power Station: Part II*, Astrup Fearnley Museum of Modern Art, Oslo, Norway
2006 *Nunca salgo sin mi cámara: Video en China*, ICO (Official Credit Institute) Collections Museum, Madrid, Spain
2006 *9th Havana Biennial*, Centro de Arte Contemporáneo Wilfredo Lam, Havana, Cuba
2005 *BEYOND: an Extraordinary Space of Experimentation for Modernization*, 2nd Guangzhou Triennial, Guangdong Museum of Art, China
2003 *Alors, la Chine?*, Centre Pompidou, Musée national d'art moderne, Paris, France
2002 *Reinterpretation: A Decade of Experimental Chinese Art (1990–2000)*, 1st Guangzhou Triennial, Guangdong Museum of Art, China

Li Ming

1986 Born in Yuan Jiang, China
2008 BFA, China Academy of Art, Hangzhou, China
Lives and works in Hangzhou, China

Selected Exhibitions

2014 *We have never participated*, 8th Shenzhen Sculpture Biennale, OCT Contemporary Art Terminal, China
2014 *PANDAMONIUM: Media Art from Shanghai*, Momentum, Berlin, Germany
2013 *28 Chinese*, Rubell Family Collection, Miami, Florida, United States
2013 *ON | OFF: China's Young Artists in Concept and Practice*, Ullens Center for Contemporary Art, Beijing, China

Liang Yue

1979 Born in Shanghai, China
2001 Fine Arts College, Shanghai University
Lives and works in Shanghai, China

Selected Exhibitions

2014 *Performance and Imagination: Photography from China 1911–2014*, Stavanger Kunstmuseum, Stavanger, Norway
2012 *Wandering Eyes: Video Art from Shanghai Exhibition*, Landesgalerie Linz, Austria
2011 *Move on Asia: The End of Video Art (2001–2010)*, Casa Asia, Barcelona, Spain
2010 *Beyond the Body – Contemporary Image Art Exhibition*, Museum of Contemporary Art, Shanghai, China
2010 *China Power Station: Part IV*, Pinacoteca Agnelli, Turin, Italy
2006 *The Thirteen: Chinese Video Now*, PS1 Contemporary Art Center, Long Island City, New York, United States
2006 *Twilight: Photography in the Magic Hour*, Victoria and Albert Museum, London, United Kingdom
2006 *Restless: Photography and New Media*, Museum of Contemporary Art, Shanghai, China
2004 *The Monk and the Demon: Contemporary Chinese Art*, Musée d'art contemporain de Lyon, France
2004 *Light as Fuck! Shanghai Assemblage 2000–2004*, Museum of Contemporary Art, National Museum of Art, Architecture and Design, Oslo, Norway
2004 *China Now*, Museum of Modern Art, New York, United States

Selected Festivals

2014 AVIFF–Art Film Festival, Cannes, France
2012 Toronto International Film Festival, Canada
2010 Yebisu International Festival for Art & Alternative Visions, Tokyo Metropolitan Museum of Photography, Japan

Liu Shiyuan

1985 Born in Beijing, China
2009 BFA, Central Academy of Fine Arts, Beijing, China
2012 MFA, School of Visual Arts, New York, United States
Lives and works in Beijing, China, and Copenhagen, Denmark

Residencies

2012 Harold Arts Residency, Columbus, Ohio, United States
2012 OCAT International Art Residency, Shenzhen, China
2014 Danish Art Workshops / Statens Værksteder for Kunst, Copenhagen, Denmark

Selected Exhibitions

2013 *Local Futures*, He Xiangning Art Museum, Shenzhen, China
2013 *Alternatives to Ritual: A Case Study of Shenzhen OCT Contemporary Art Terminal*, OCT Contemporary Art Terminal, Shenzhen, China
2012 *7th Shenzhen Sculpture Biennale*, OCT Contemporary Art Terminal, Shenzhen, China
2011 *stillspotting nyc*, organized by the Solomon R. Guggenheim Museum, New York, United States

Sun Xun

1980 Born in Fuxin, China
2005 Graduated from Printmaking Department of China Academy of Art, Hangzhou, China
Lives and works in Beijing, China

Selected Exhibitions

2014 *Sun Xun: Yesterday is Tomorrow*, Hayward Gallery, London, United Kingdom
2014 *A Time for Dreams*, 4th Moscow International Biennale for Young Art, Russia
2014 *Myth/History: Yuz Collection of Contemporary Art*, Yuz Museum, Shanghai, China
2014 *15 Years Chinese Contemporary Art Award (CCAA)*, Power Station of Art, Shanghai, China
2014 *Video Art at the Dr. Bhau Daji Lad Museum*, Mumbai, India
2013 *The Garden of Diversion*, Sifang Art Museum, Nanjing, China
2013 *China China: Individuality–Collective*, PinchukArtCentre, Kiev, Ukraine
2013 *ON | OFF: China's Young Artists in Concept and Practice*, Ullens Center for Contemporary Art, Beijing, China
2012 7th Asia Pacific Triennial of Contemporary Art (APT7), Gallery of Modern Art and Queensland Art Gallery, Brisbane, Australia
2012 *4th Taipei International Modern Ink Painting Biennial*, Tai-chung, Taipei, and Tao-yüan, Taiwan
2012 *Modern Monsters / Death and Life of Fiction*, Taipei Biennial 2012, Taipei Fine Arts Museum and The Paper Mill, Taiwan
2012 *The Unexpected Guest*, Liverpool Biennial 2012, The Bluecoat, United Kingdom

2011 *Moving Image in China: 1988–2011*, Minsheng Art Museum, Shanghai, China
2011 *OUR MAGIC HOUR: How Much of the World Can We Know?*, Yokohama Triennale 2011, Yokohama Museum of Art, Japan
2008 *Sun Xun: The New China*, Hammer Museum, Los Angeles, United States

Selected Festivals and Screenings

2014 The Floating Cinema 2014, presentation organized by Centre for Chinese Contemporary Art, London, United Kingdom
2014 17th Holland Animation Film Festival, Utrecht, Netherlands
2014 43rd International Film Festival Rotterdam, Netherlands
2013 8th International Rome Film Festival, Italy
2013 13th Seoul International NewMedia Festival, Korea
2013 30th Busan International Short Film Festival, Korea
2013 Kino Der Kunst, Munich, Germany
2013 37th Hong Kong International Film Festival, Hong Kong
2012 London International Animation Festival, London, United Kingdom
2012 Kuandu International Animation Festival, Taipei, Taiwan
2010 *Clown's Revolution*, Holland Animation Film Festival, Centraal Museum, Utrecht, Netherlands
2009 *Moving Perspectives: Shahzia Sikander/Sun Xun*, Arthur M. Sackler Gallery, Smithsonian Institution, Washington, D.C., United States
2008 *In-Between: Asian Video Art Weekend*, Mori Art Museum, Tokyo, Japan
2007 *Sun Xun: Art Didn't Have a Standard*, 12+Contemporary Film Screening of Experimental Animation, Museum of Contemporary Art, Shanghai, China

Wang Xin

1983 Born in Yichang, China
2010 BFA, China Academy of Art, Hangzhou, China
2012 MFA, School of the Art Institute of Chicago, United States
Lives and works in Shanghai, China

Selected Exhibitions

2014 *Rediscovery*, Animamix Biennale 2013–2014, Museum of Contemporary Art, Shanghai, China
2010 *Beyond the Body: Contemporary Image Art Exhibition*, Museum of Contemporary Art, Shanghai, China
2010 *Get It Louder 2010*, Sanlitun SOHO, Beijing, China

Selected Festivals and Screenings

2014 Chinese Visual Festival, Anatomy Theater & Museum, King's College London, United Kingdom
2012 1st Shenzhen Independent Animation Biennale, Shenzhen Overseas Chinese Creative Park Area, China
2011 Musrara Mix Festival, Jerusalem, Israel

SELECTED BIBLIOGRAPHY

Bao Dong, Pu Hong, Sun Dongdong, Philip Tinari, Paula Tsai, and Laura Tucker. *ON | OFF: China's Young Artists in Concept & Practice*. Exhibition catalogue. Beijing: Ullens Center for Contemporary Art, Hinabook, and World Publishing Company, 2013.

Chiu, Melissa, and Miwako Tezuka. *Yang Fudong: Seven Intellectuals in a Bamboo Forest.* Exhibition catalogue. New York: Asia Society Museum, 2009.

Dal Lago, Francesca, Paul Gladston, Pauline J. Yao, and Huang Zhuan. *Zhang Peili: Certain Pleasures*. Edited by Venus Lau and Robin Peckham. Exhibition catalogue. Hong Kong: Blue Kingfisher Limited, 2011.

Elaine, James and Su Wei. *Perspectives 180 - Unfinished Country: New Video from China*. Exhibition catalogue. Houston: Contemporary Arts Museum Houston, 2012.

He Juxing, Guo Xiaoyan, and Zhou Tiehai. *Moving Image in China 1988–2011*. Exhibition catalogue. Shanghai: Minsheng Art Museum, 2011.

Hu Xiaoyuan. *Hu Xiaoyuan*. Exhibition catalogue. Beijing: Beijing Commune, 2010.

Joo, Eungie. *The Ungovernables: The 2012 New Museum Triennial*. Exhibition catalogue. New York: Skira Rizzoli and New Museum, 2012.

Lu Peng. *A History of Art in 20th-Century China*. Milan: Charta, 2010.

Reifenscheid, Beate, ed. *China's ReVision*. Exhibition catalogue. Munich, London and New York: Prestel, 2008.

Roselione-Valadez, Juan, ed. *28 Chinese: Rubell Family Collection*. Exhibition catalogue. Miami: Rubell Family Collection, 2014.

Sans, Jérôme, and Guo Xiaoyan. *Breaking Forecast: 8 Key Figures of China's New Generation Artists*. Exhibition catalogue. Hong Kong: Blue Kingfisher Limited, 2010.

Sans, Jérôme. *China Talks: Interviews with 32 Contemporary Artists by Jérôme Sans*. Edited by Chen Yun and Michelle Woo; translated by Chen Yun and Philip Tinari. Hong Kong: Timezone 8 Limited, 2009.

Smith, Karen. *Nine Lives: The Birth of Avant-garde Art in New China*. New York: AW Asia, 2008.

Wu Hung, and Christopher Phillips. *Between Past and Future: New Photography and Video from China*. Exhibition catalogue. Chicago: David and Alfred Smart Museum of Art, University of Chicago; New York: International Center of Photography; and Göttingen, Germany: Steidl, 2004.

CONTRIBUTORS

Melissa Chiu is Director of the Asia Society Museum, New York.

Tony Guerrero is Executive and Artistic Director, Whitebox Art Center, New York.

Chrissie Iles is Anne and Joel Ehrenkranz Curator, Whitney Museum of American Art, New York.

Dr. Michael I. Jacobs is an art collector, physician, and Associate Clinical Professor of Dermatology, Weill Medical College of Cornell University, New York.

Robin Peckham is deputy editor of *LEAP* in Beijing and chief editor of *The Art Newspaper* in Hong Kong.

Published in 2014 to accompany the exhibition
Now You See: New Chinese Video Art
from the Collection of Dr. Michael I. Jacobs,
on view May 25–June 19, 2014

Whitebox Art Center
329 Broome Street
New York, NY 10002
whiteboxny.org

ISBN 978-0-9905366-0-4

Project managed by Tammy Leung, RN BSN
Edited by Beth Turk
Designed by Miko McGinty, Yoonjung Choi,
    Kaegan Sparks, and Claire Bidwell

Printed and bound in Italy by Trifolio SRL, Verona

cover: **Cheng Ran.** *The Sorrows of Young Werther*, 2009 (detail).
4-channel color video, sound. 10:12 min.
page 2: **Sun Xun.** *Beyond-ism*, 2010 (detail). Single-channel
color video, sound. 8:08 min.
page 6: **Cheng Ran.** *Anonymity, or Imitation and Imagining of*
Man Ray's Tears (1930–1932), 2010 (detail). Single-channel
color video, sound. 15 min.
page 15: **Sun Xun.** *People's Republic of Zoo*, 2009 (detail).
Single-channel color video, sound. 7:30 min.